H.E.R.

Heaven's Epitome Realized

An Ode To The Black Woman

By

Dominic McDonald, Sean Cook, and Edward A. Ellis II

Table Of Contents

Dear Black Woman,

I wish that I didn't hate that I love you because I should love to love you. We are in a state of emergency with each other because our union is being attacked by oppressors. The media has you out here assimilating to an aesthetic that is foreign to your history and design. Lines are being blurred between what makes you comfortable in your own skin and what gets you vain attention and notoriety. I can't tell what's genuine and what's made up. Therefore my main message is to discover who you are and be that no matter what. Never shrink yourselves because you feel that you don't belong. You birthed this Earth - we inhabit it together.

You are whatever you say you are because you have the divine authority to do so. Your words like the wind can be sweet and breezy or firm and gusty. Your body like the ocean can make gentle waves or crash upon the shore. Your soul like the earth can be soft as sand or hard as clay. My wish is that this project speaks life into you. I hope that you can gain something from the point of views from three different perspectives of three ages of millennial black males.

I feel that *H.E.R* is needed in times of today's social America where Black Women are looking for support and comfort from their men. The pieces in this book are here to inspire, empower, and entertain. Please let them be received with an open heart and open mind. I love you all.
Yours always,

Dominic "Nerd" McDonald

I Would Give you

If I could give you something you could have forever,
I would give you my smile
My memory foam lips
Reveal my cross biting teeth that,
Through God's mercy stay in tact
Because I haven't been to the dentist since 19
Groomed by Crest,
Sometimes with whitening,
Sometimes wintergreen fresh
And of course the dimples. Scientifically
Known as birth defects but a sign
From the Lord that there is beauty
In things that seem imperfect
All these are a brand, burned
In your thoughts of me
And let it warm you just the same
When frowns plague our minutes
And pouts ruin our days
Keep this with you infinitely
So that even in heaven's home
You may still be able to recognize me.

- Dominic "Nerd" McDonald

Can't Be Photoshopped

Your soul can not be photoshopped
As if you in your entirety could be fully contained
In pixels .jpeg or .pdf frames
It would take virtual reality, 3-D holograms
For anyone to even think about beginning to understand
And surprisingly Apple nor Microsoft has not made the technology
I'm sure if they did then they are saving it for the iPhone 23
You shouldn't be so used to being behind screens
Basically it takes more than a picture to be received.
The cover ups of your bruises and blemishes
Fast forward past the stories
Color pops don't quite deliver the correct frequencies
Not downing you for being a canvas of aesthetics
It would just be neat to see, the real you
And experience how another being
Doesn't technically enter your body but still fills you
I want my heart touched by your talent
I want my mind to be amazed by what your skills do
And maybe even, when you enter the room,
Have parts of me feel how roller coaster ride thrills move.
What's seen on the outside temporarily prevails
Show your soul as often as you show your shell.

- Dominic "Nerd" McDonald

Fan To a Nobody

To the one who sat too close to the stage
there but still distant, telescope perspectives
allowed you to perceive receiving
recognition to someone who
doesn't know you but your shadow
is familiar. Darkened by an ambiance
to make the star look brighter,
however it is still stuck in the lonely space.
You invaded me in my alienation.
But it wasn't for domination,
maybe not from the start,
because my heart you did take over on the sly
you won't admit to it and I can't admit
why I let you - in that space I should have left you.
But there is a cold fact about isolation,
things move slower at cooler temperatures.
A star, is bright and hot, so when we meet
we'll be doing things far from chillin',
because you dared to touch what
many believed could not be handled
and remembered my calculated location
even when I was cloaked
In the daylight. For that I thank you.
Hope you're not too disappointed
when the stage is gone, and I'm not even what these
dim lights and spotlight make me to be.
When I'm just like you.

- Dominic "Nerd" McDonald

I Just Want You To Love Me

I just want you to love me,
Like when you see
your food coming to you at a restaurant.
You've read about me, asked for recommendations
Looked at what I was made of
… maybe or maybe not seen a picture first.
But you know I am going to satisfy your emptiness
And fill you up even though it hasn't happened yet
If I am too much, you can always
Get a to-go box. Love me like
Fresh out of the dryer socks
Giving you tingling sensations at your foundations
And with you every step of the way
I protect you and in return
You try your best to keep me clean ,unstained ,
avoiding the damage the outside world is ready to give
me.
Or, a cool breeze
On a hot day at the beach
While you're eating ice cream
Or sucking down a Slurpee
Slowly so that you don't get a brain freeze
Feel me, against you but
Still with you, naturally
As if it were how things are supposed to be …

- Dominic "Nerd" McDonald

Beauty and the Geek

Now I know we don't associate
but this might stop the presses.
Your gorgeous frame and gorgeous face
has lead me to confessions.
That come from the heart and mind
I would like to reach,
not the singer or rapper kind
my passion is to teach.
No fashion designer,
or professional photographer.
More aerospace engineering,
having buildings modeled up.
You got the smooth Agents at the club talking game,
I can explain graphic design
and how a game is made.
Dudes wanna take you down and show you off in public.
I wanna take you up, and show you what real love is,
and if you're not in magazines
I'll wake up to you in my sheets.
If opposites attract, will you be
the beauty to my geek?

- Dominic "Nerd" McDonald

Distant Lover

Numbers of miles in the thousands
Got us segregated
Moments to whiles to months to years
Since we've embraced in
Relations & things that keep us separated
Since plane tickets and frequent flyer miles
To me are a foreign language.
If only my Hughes was Howard
And not Langston
Or I could work enough for paid vacations
I would exercise my rights for visitations
With you, there would be no delays to lay with
LA has opportunities but they
are hidden with agendas.
She moved for school so her resume
Could make her a better contender
Maybe she'll come back for the Summer
Or for Thanksgiving in November
Or to escape the cold of the east coast winter
Now I'm on Tinder, swiping left and right
But I still can't find a match
To the flame you would ignite
It's 7:00pm here, 10:00pm there
So I figure I'll text her goodnight
All my distant lovers, only time will tell
If we reunite.

- Dominic "Nerd" McDonald

Vegetables

Ma'am is ya,
Bruce Banner unhappy?
Cause you got a mean walk
I'm feeling taller than
Whats at the end of Jack's bean stalk
And I would invest green stock
In anything that you give effort to
If it's something you
don't like I say "eff it" too.
I shouldn't want you, but
You're good for me like vegetables
Your meaning in my life
Is just what the doctor ordered, unlegible
Yet without you I'm dark and blue
Like what's bottled by PepsiCo.
So I'm here flesh and bone
Meeting you at the crossroad
Wishing for you with crossed fingers
And even crossed toes.

- Dominic "Nerd" McDonald

Lovely Lady Lava Lamp

Be my lovely lady lava lamp.
I can stare at you for hours
you can make things move
while standing still, like a special power.
Not too much and not too little
like to see it shake, like to see it jiggle
your company is appreciated, though
you can't stay, but it's the reason
I have no problem when you walk away.
You're my lovely lady lava lamp
not too soft not too firm
if it's too much to handle
then I'm willing to learn.
It might take you half a day,
to make a full turn.
Some might walk and some might chase
to see how it sticks out and claims its space.
It's a lovely lady lava lamp.
God's gift to the land
something that I appreciate
while most don't understand
Just look at what was done
to Sara Baartman.
Moves in circles, moves in waves
if you give it to me I won't misbehave
I would take good care,
and I would spend the day.
I would always be fair
because I would like to play,
with my lovely lady lava lamp.

- Dominic "Nerd" McDonald

Cuddle Season

The atmosphere is becoming discomforting
buff and brawny clouds bully the sun away
gray is the day as stone cold oxygen
chills our deep breaths and out
blows smoke without the use of cigarettes.
And no fire will turn you to ash
like the dry air that comes when it's 7pm passed,
It's Cuddle Season.
After spring flings flew and summer flips flopped
you start to get jealous of the hands on your watch
cause they are not on you.
Materials of cotton and polyester are breached
by icy air that clenches the teeth
we cover of flesh geese and seek
another source of heat,
it's Cuddle Season.
She was sad to be single for the holidays,
around Halloween everyone looking for a boo.
Might be a ghost but at least they come through.
May not be real but you believe it's true.
She'll fill your calendar 'til the year is new
hoping you're able, she didn't cook this year
but she'll bring a man to the table, then afterwards
it's On Demand cable, Blockbuster night, or Netflix.
Dinner by Six, wine by Nine, and done by One
cause she gotta be at work in the morning.
It's Cuddle Season ...
If Blackplanet was still in she'd send a Note,
if Myspace was still in she'd post a Bulletin,
yet today her Facebook status brings sadness
and while men can comment,
they never seem to replace the e-n with I.
Relationships are on a hiring freeze,
but she does accept applications
just to put her mind at ease,
hoping to schedule some interviews right before
February 14th.
But don't get cocky, for its cold outside
and you're just a warm body.
See when the draft kicks,
in come the draft picks

and she scouts,
tryna get you to devour her Thin Mints.
Please, do use discretion,
or it will be on to the next one, cause
it's Cuddle Season!

- Dominic "Nerd" McDonald

If You Are Alone Tonight

If you are alone tonight, you are with the greatest person
you know.
For I cannot love you
if you do not love yourself.

We treat our bed and couch spaces as obligations
for someone to occupy.
Not knowing why or caring for that matter.
What matters is that we need someone to listen
to the voice's in our head
to soothe the aches of our pains
to put the missing pieces together
us incomplete as sentence fragments
when writing our autobiographies.
Getting to the point so we can know that a happy ever
will be after.
I come from a planet,
where we take access for granted.
Ignoring our incompletions but demanding
something picture perfect
without the right mind frame.
Finding a short in our wires trying to connect
to something greater - just won't work.
So if you are alone tonight, realize that you are with the
greatest person
you'll ever know, for I cannot love you
if you do not love yourself.

- Dominic "Nerd" McDonald

Dear Black Women,

I love you with a passion. You're strength and grace can't be described and we as Black Men appreciate it. I hope you can sense my enthusiasm and endearment for you through the words beyond this page. Welcome to H.E.R.

  - Sean Cook

Black Girl Magic

Sprinkled in pixie dust
Or more like sand from the Kalahari desert
Inequivalent to 3 wishes out a genie naw this is much better
Rubbing over lamps or prayers sent to heaven
Can't get it like rabbits out of a hat
Maybe if you ring out a badu rap over the top of some melanin
Its heaven sent
You gotta grin
Ain't too much better than
Staring in
The brown eyed reflection
Of a Queen stronger than Ms. Honeybee in a Black Dynamite fiction
More beautiful than a Dorothy Dandridge and a Nefertiti mixture
Skin of bronze and hair of wool they essence is depicted in scripture
It paints a picture so drastic
So fantastic
It'slike the sun kissed version of Disney's Fantasmic
Something so dope it can only be described as
Black Girl Magic
Fuck, just imagine
It's how black don't crack mixed with a whole lot of passion
Its elegance and style mixed with a whole lot of fashion
Its kinky curly, coconut oil, and shea butter
Black Girls sparkling like magic
They say this sparkle is just a glimmer of everything that describes our women's universal awesomeness
They bossyness
They confidence
When they walk with a switch
They lips be juicy and voluptuous
They I just left the shop and my eyebrows on fleek got me feeling saucy shit
They be talking shit
Nagging you in the kitchen but you love they spirit
Or women like Maya Angelou, Harriet Tubman, and Serena Williams, shit you gotta love they spirit
Or like when Ms. Upile Chisala said "I Am Dripping In Melanin and Honey. I am Black Without Apology"

You betta talk that shit
Yea we love it
Aint nothing above it
They power and resilience
They so amazing its surreal and
I don't know how to describe they dopeness
It's hopeless
I'm choking
In the face of this
This goddess of the sun
With her natural hair in a bun
Baby hair laid in the front
And her face beat to the Gawds
Got my pulse pulsating odd
Jumping like Jiminy Cricket or like my heart playing leap frog
This goes out to all my beautiful black queens
I wanna salute yall and give you a round of applause
And I just thank god
For Black Girl Magic

- *S.P.J.*

Soulmate

I done seen reflections of sky's and oceans
Pairs that reciprocate each individuals interior motives
Its bodies like this that create this itch this glitch this twitch of
an emotion
My heart beating, beats like the root of a vegetable
Tapping snares to connect wit you
Like Dre sponsored this connection
So it's wireless range is inseparable
I feel it wherever
Whenever
Whatever this is I can't explain
However you frame it
I'll claim it
I just know it's like a sensation I've never felt before
Like this warmth I feel even when the winter wind blows
Tears of laughter as we talking about growing old
Wrapped in kisses that ignites us both
Sex feeling like I reached through your stomach and we linked
soul to soul
You curl yo toes
Sweat dripping from my nose
You're an angel and I just thought you should know
I've never met someone more amazing
It's crazy
This aphrodisiacal passion
This thrilling desire that latched us
The most beautiful sight, there's nothing you don't have
Cute lip, nice legs and a sexy little ass
I love the way you smile and how you laugh
I can tell how you think and act
That our mind soul and bodies match
They done latched
We attached
We reciprocate each other even when we aren't where the
other one is at
I've never experienced a mirrored and rangeless reflection
like that
You're an angel sent from heaven's gate
My Queen, My Boo, My Bae, My Ace
You're my soulmate
- *S.P.J.*

Hopeless

I know this girl
This beautiful black girl
With long nappy hair
Light brown eyes
And she seemed hopeless
We locked eyes
And talked for only a moment but seemed to be a lifetime
Her eyes were brown but soon turned blue due to the bodies of
water that she tried to hold back but just couldn't
The ocean that cascaded into a hurricane and broke the Levi's
that she called eyelids
She wore this hoodie
It had the hood hovered over her face and laced hiding her
soul
Like curtains in front of her self-esteem that was too low to
stand and allow her to love herself
And this girl
Who's heart was as light as a feather but wasn't very strong
Looked me in the eye
And she allowed me to see into her soul
It was as shattered as an iPhone screen
That fell flat on its face from the top of the Twin Towers
It was broken she lost all hope
She said she had been praying to a god for too long
N for too long she heard no response
She had faith that was drawn in a trace book and erased as
easily as a child's first mistake
She was searching for something she thought could never be
obtained so she prayed
And hoped her prayers would lead to better days
But they didn't
Cuz when she spoke
It sounded like a pack of wolves howling for salvation toward
the moon
She said
I just want somebody to love me
I told her I said
My sister
You beautiful black queen
Remove your hood
And wipe your eyes

Open your heart n soul
You hold your head high
And you love yourself
You love yourself like a queen
And your king will come to you
Don't settle for less than you deserve
And your birth right on the lowest level is a man that will trust
you
He will respect and love you
And I said
love, dont give up
You see I know it's hard
I'm searching too

- *S.P.J.*

Eyes Bluer Than Mine

Yo I've seen eyes bluer than mine
Black skin
Sometimes lighter but mostly the pigment is a bit darker
They heart beats harder
Born to be martyrs
It's in they nature
Divine straight from our creator
And if it's heaven sent then who are we to debate it
Our back bones
Our future
The shit that holds us together when we fall apart like the
London Bridge
And since we've been kids
born n raised lied to
Unwillingly closing our eyes seemingly to be blind
But are you listening
Can you hear me
Where would we be without our black women
See I couldn't even imagine or fathom
The devastation we would be in
They keep us strong in our moments of weakness
We need it
In willie lynch's speech making of a slave
He states
The most important thing is controlling the women
If she don't support the man he's weaker
Then she influences the children so the disconnect grows
deeper
Ain't that some shit
How the white man know the key to our salvation
But black folk
Sitting around holding hands praying
Waiting on Jesus to come fix our messed up generation
Get off your knees from praying
And crack the foundation on which you're stationed
Break barriers of sexist ideology
And rupture your thoughts like earthquakes in Haiti
It's crazy
Yo it's crazy how our generation
Has dehumanized our queens
Men treat women as if they own them

Possessive nightmare
Kinda reminds me of slavery
It's said that they only worth something if they back is bent
And I'll tell you after our daughters turn to women that's how
half of their life is spent
Cause it's hard to keep you vertebrae straight when it's
constantly holding up 6 times its weight
Amazing
They modern day saviors
Bearing the cross of all those around them
Who can't carry their own weight
But Black men can't be the spear that stabs them in the rib
We were made to support each other
Men at the head and women pulled from his side to be equal
Its evil
How we are internally perceived
How we gonna fight injustice
If our own communities is fucked up
We gotta love each other
These black women got blue eyes
Cuz they all teary eyed cause we don't respect them enough
As if they weren't born into a society that's already tough
How much pain can your heart take
Before it starts to break
Like the Levi's when Katrina came knocking at its front gate
Everyday we gotta deal with white supremacy and racism
But they can't even come home to they so called man and get
confirmation that they a symbol of greatness
And I hate it
How we gonna fix the outside world
And our inside is so tainted
If we are gonna build we gotta start from the roots
Beneath the surface of the floor
We gotta love and respect our women more
we gotta hold they hands
we gotta open the doors for them
It's the little shit

We gotta reinforce the culture of our women being priceless
Yo it's a cycle
We start to treat our women as good as what they are really
worth
Then that gives birth to them treating us like kings
And then our children see it and do the same damn thing
And it just repeats itself
Generation to generation
And this love will create a nation
Where our women are sacred
We gotta realize loving our women is the secret to our peoples
salvation

S.P.J.

3 Lined Poem

A conversation with the first girl I saw after Cupid
shot me with his arrow
Hi...
I've never really been good at saying what's on my
heart so I usually say what's on my mind
But there's something different about this time
See this time
I feel like I'm going crazy
Like there's a war in my stomach
And the message that it's sending to my brain
It's contradicting the way my body has been trained
to maintain
It feels like there's an alien army attacking causing
tornadoes and tsunamis
Washing up islands and countries
Destroying oak and palm trees
Massacring birds and bumble bees
Even the caterpillars die
And it's fucked up that they will never get the chance
to turn into butterflies
And the.....
Damn I guess you can say that I caught a case of the
Butterflies
Nervous like the birds and the bees
Palms sweating like tsunamis
And what's really crazy is if you think about it the
only thing that I've said to her so far is hi
I've never felt this before
It's like my whole life I've been dead
And now I'm finally alive
Like it took 21 years for me to find the perfect bride
We can be like Adam and Eve
Except there's no snake no garden of Eden and no
apple on a tree
We can be like Romeo n Juliet
Except were black
And ain't no black people gonna drink poison to be
together
See they took the easy way out
It only took them a second to die for each other
But living for each other is gonna take us a life time

I only plan on doing this once so this has to be the right time
That fucking Arrow gave me tunnel vision and you're the only one in my sight line
And now She just staring at me cuz I'm standing here and I still ain't hit her with a punch line....
Hi... I just got shot with an arrow
And Now she thinks I'm fucking crazy
Cuz I just told her I got shot with an arrow
My next line has to be more thought out because I'm starting to look like a bit of a weirdo
Maybe I'll tell her about herself
I should've done that two lines ago
I'll tell her about her eyes and how they shine like the moon and the stars
Or how every time she blinks
my jaw drops making a noise that sounds like a cymbal on a brand new drum set
how the pulse in my veins pick up and sounds like when that snare hits
My heart beats loud like the bass
Yea that mutha fucka legit with the sticks
See her eyelashes are like the conductor to the dopest beat
That even God would nod his head to while he played it on repeat
Our love could be amazing
Or maybe I'll talk about her smile
And how it's the most gorgeous thing I've seen in a while
Or how it can even brighten up the darkest of skies
Naw those are just some weak ass punch lines
Imma talk about her
But fucks she's perfect
My thoughts can't be worded
But I just gotta find a few things to say and hopefully I don't get wordy
Cause I could go on and on
Everything about her is amazing
Meeting a modern day queen is so rare
She should have a more visible crown attached to her head
Like the curls on her head

Jesus Her fucking hair
I love her hair
Every single strand connects to her scalp
Once I stood behind her and I caught a whiff of her
scent
It hit me right in the snout
It was amazing
It resembled the sensation of an oceanic sky
Lit up by the sun at the peak of its rise
Covered by dandelions blossoming in the spring
It was like the opening scene in Bambi
That shit was beautiful
I just want to let you know you're beautiful
Fuck I'm pitiful
"Hi"
"I just got shot with an arrow"
"I just want to let you know You're beautiful"
Worst 3 lines I've said in my life
Someone tell Cupid if he shoots with an arrow
It should come with a complimentary poem for you to
recite
Instead I'm standing here like a deer in fucking
headlights
Just breathe

....

Hi
Sometimes... Sometimes I wish I could find the right
words to say what's on my heart
But instead I usually say what's on my mind
But see this time
They seem to be intertwined
And I just want to let you know I.....

S.P.J.

<u>Summertime Chill</u>

It gets hella cold in the summertime
Eyes open wide I can't seem to sleep at night
Tossing and turning
It's the way my heart beat
Pumping and shifting gears down the street
Its tryna get to you
398 miles from my house
to your apartment complex by the California state
It's irate how this shit make my heart feel faint
It's sorta like when I was next to
you stretched across my chest
I was trying not to move
Mesmerized by your afro sheen
And your beautiful brown melanin
Wrap up I settled in
The intoxication of sheets
The toxin seeped into my pours
It's like you were 100 proof
and my livers were new to this
I couldn't even be around you
without getting love drunk
I was drunk off you
My eyes got blurry
But I remember holding you
Your lips touching mine
Sucking your mouth dry
As I drank your secretion
To better help me digest your secrets
You didn't have the terminology to articulate
But the sentiment to surmise
It was like kissing May for the first time
But chills of winter running down my spine
It gets hella cold in the summertime
Like snow storm in the mountains
When it hits your face the pain
It's so painful
Your touch on my face it's so painful
Cuz it's so temporary I know I can't sustain it
like a butterfly in the wind
it's hard to capture
and I knew it was bad the morning after

when I leaned in for a kiss
but it was more like a disaster
your face calling me a stranger
at that moment I realized I had to
rearrange the emotion in my chest
and the tone in my voice
I had to appear as if you weren't
leaving me vacant
I was broken
And I'll tell you
The most fucked up part about feelings is
when you aren't able to feel it
You gotta push emotion to the side and
write it down to reveal it
It gets hella fucking cold in the summertime
I just wanna hold you
Staring at your soul
From the connection I made by glancing
through your open window
It looks like a mirror
I can see myself
It's a reflection of the future
Hell you gimme a crystal ball
N I'll tell you it all
It's about us
All we gotta do is build a little trust
And set a foundation strong enough for us
to set the pyramids on
See it's written in your eyes
N it gets hella cold in the summertime
Freezing shifting from side to side
Sorta like a sway
Reminded me of the day
You stretched out your hand
And we moved to the most amazing beat
I think it's hella funny that you're a dancer
n I got 2 left feet
I reminisce on you wrapped in my arms
As we moved to the rhythm of your heart
Everything about you sang to me

But sometimes that's all you need
Is a voice of reason to keep you warm in the storm
It gets hella cold in the summertime
It gets so fucking cold without you sometimes
It don't make no sense to be cold when it's 100 degrees outside
See I just wish you were here
Cuz without you I'm so cold on the inside

- *S.P.J.*

Edith Of Eden

So y'all know I be on Instagram straight flexin
And if y'all don't follow me I apologize your life is probably
depressing
But look
I was online one day and I was presented with a task
To group rate some chicks based of the beauty of the face
And the fluff of they ass
But check me
My cousin sent a pic of this one meezy
And I was thinking
Yo I've seen her somewhere
It was her smile
And so I went to Instagram and it took me a while
But I found her
And when I found her I saw her name was Edith
It made me think of Eden
Then it hit me
It was our past life
This Edith is a reincarnation of my wife
When I saw her last
I was Adam and she was eve
And I'm pretty sure we were under the forbidden tree
Doing forbidden things
And before you get some sexual imagery
I swear to you we were just picking fruit
You see we were just making a fruit basket for my father
It was his gift
It was his gift for her lips
The way he precisely constructed them from a nimbus cloud
And it was crazy how our peaceful world got chaotically loud
When mine met with hers
And my father being the architect that his is
Realized he may have made the sun too bright
So he took some of its light n placed it in her
Now she can luminate even the darkest rooms when her lips
part
He felt I wasn't adequately using my heart
So on the fateful day when he placed his hands on earth
And pulled her from my rib
He did it so I could love her
I knew we would live together for forever

But see forever never seemed so close to never
See we ate some fruit from my fathers basket
And it was the last thing we saw before our caskets
See we died
And she rose to the sky
While I fell to the wayside
See I wasn't strong enough to hold her hand
To hold it steady when the snake temped her with his plans
His tactics of manipulation was too heavy
And it caused her to break down and collapse like two towers
on 9/11
And I was suppose to catch her
But I didn't
See since it was my fault
she rose to heaven
And I fell to the side
But soon I was reborn as a butterfly
But I died
Then I molded and formed into an oak tree
And after about 500 years
They cut me down and I fell into the ocean
See I turned into a tortoise
And that was my life before this one
And it's kinda funny because I can still feel the turtle like
symptoms
But see now I'm human
And believe me Edith I'm sorry
I apologize that my father had to clip your wings and discard
your halo so you could live a life where u encountered me
Yo In your presence I'm left breathless
And I've been stressing
Because you probably are thinking you don't even know me
But I was cursed with remembering
See I've spent the last 1000 years waiting to hear the
symphony of your voice again
See I've been forced to live in a world without you

And now that I've found you
I never wanna leave you
And please I know how this sounds
And I see you are reluctant to believe me
But we've been connect by our lips
My father constructed us to be drawn together by our kiss
It's his gift to us
But I'll earn your trust
So just give me a chance
And you'll see when our lips touch

- *S.P.J.*

The Greatest Love Story Never Told

I told myself I wasn't gonna do this no mo
Not gon lie and say I never felt like this before
Cuz I don lived long enough to feel this many times and more
But something about this feel different
Got my heart fluttering off beat some shit feel tricky
Using my hands tryna piece together the dots
tryna figure out shit what's good wit me
Too many times I drop poems and lines
That caress a woman's mind
But don't stand the test of time
Just me auctioning off my heart for less than a dime
Just a quick dope ass rhyme
For another female who's divine
Then I find myself back here
On this stage just me and a mic
Shit looking in a mirror asking myself if this is what life is like
A feature film movie
With a small ole cast and a whole lot of bloopers
Shit I'm a trooper
But if I can set the scene with the first few words that come to
my mind like we sitting in yo home girl house around a twisted
dime
Scene 1
Set stage
It's embarking on the night time
Just me n you I'm holding yo hand listening to slow jams
While we sipping on some white wine
Im staring in your eyes
I see the Orange and blue sky's
with a couple of grey lines
as the sun starts to set
And those clouds start to clear
I see the constellations brightly shining
And the full moons right behind them
After time fades it's becoming a new day
So the sun starts to rise and we see the mornings red sky
And I look at it as it kisses your skin from yo neck to yo thigh
I just wish I had the heart to say what's on my mind,
like my chest beats my vocal cord till I bleed the right line
But instead I just stare at you rather than telling you you're
beautiful

And don't act like this is new to you
I told you I been a fan since you first popped up out the Sands
When I first glanced at yo face
I felt Goofy like Max singing after today
And you were Roxanne
I tripped and couldn't stand
Tumbling down the stands
rolling over a group of trash cans
My face hit the sand
I fell for you
Like golden brown leaves in climax of autumn days
I'm dazed
Star gazed
Shits real blurry out my left and my right eye
Starting to see yo freckles looking like constellations in the sky
I'm looking like Harriet Tubman in 1855
Naturally they guide me to you
But I don't have a burning passion for freedom
This just my heart catching fire
This more like the Bob Marley writing music after he wakes up
and gets high
Like the sun rise with the warm orange sky
Kinda like your skins accent from your neck to yo thighs
Then zoom the camera out and pan to the side
Cut
Imma call the first scene legendary music in the sky
You see I feel like I can never dream too high
Now let's see what the next scene gon be like
Action
Scene 2
The setting is in constant motion
I'm getting to really know you
We back to reality
I'm choking on gravity
It seems to have locked me into this particular stance and I
can't move
I fathom it's a bittersweet hell
Locked up like lazareth
This labyrinth of my dreams
Where you haunt me
You tease me
You've placed me in a small cage and I can't leave it
Nawing at the gates like a toddler teething

I'm tryna taste freedom
My heart is palpitating
Like my chest 2 15s in the back of a chevy the whole block
hear it beating
Jaw locked tongue twisted can't really speak
I feel like my tongue bench pressing soliloquies
I'm feeling claustrophobic I can hardly breathe
It's hard to see
And
Cut
Imma call the second scene friend zoned
with no perception of freedom
Been trapped in my thoughts and lost in my dreams
But seeing them in life you realize it ain't as easy as you
dreamed it
Sometimes you gotta give up and just be there if needed
So I'm done
I've conceded
Mentally I'm defeated
But my heart still craving you like a needle to a fiend
So maybe "The Druggy" will be the title of 3RD scene
Action
I'm addicted to your passion
Zoom in
Everything spoken like a queen where even when she's wrong
you believe she's taking the right action
Now lets get an up and down pan in
Your sex appeal comes from you being an aggressive savage
Fade into a flash back dream sequence
It's like you princess jasmine and I'm Aladdin
I recognize your godliness and I'm just tryna match it
Now fade out the dream and zoom in the camera quick
I'm caught up staring at yo face hoping one day I'm worthy of
grabbing it
Pulling you close and biting yo bottom lip kinda how you do it
but a bit more passionate
I imagine it to be immaculate
Zoom out to a voice over of me saying
But that's all I can do is imagine it
Cut
And here I am once again
On this stage
Just me and a mic

Shit looking at yall asking myself if this movie really what my life is like

- *S.P.J.*

Hopeless SecretsPt. 2

I should've loved you
I should've taken the time to get to know you
To blow the dust off of the story of your life that you had been
hiding under the skeletons in your closet
Open your life story and see what was causing you all this
pain
But I didn't
I was too afraid of the commitment
Never found time to stand by your side and look into your eyes
See now I know you're afraid of the light
You hide in the shadows of the darkness
Afraid that someone might see into your soul and feel your
pain
I should've helped you
I should've been that shoulder for you to cry on
I never knew all the things that you were hiding
If only you would've stepped into the light and showed me
your secrets
Allowed me to strengthen your weakness
I could've been there to help you survive

- *S.P.J.*

Sitting at the bar
Thirsting for liquor
Looking to my left I see something brown that's tempting
I grab it by the bottom Im careful not to waste it
Holding it by the throat, my lips on the rim I can taste it
Drink it to the last drop
Damn I just faced it
I cant face it
How often do our women get used like they were brewed in
barrel of some shit we made with a label
Sitting at the bar
Thirsting for her attention
Right to my left a sistah who's brown and tempting
Graze her bottom and hold her waist without being given
permission
After a few drinks and short sentences
Grab her throat and kiss her neck and lips
Afterwards we cant even look them in the face we just dismiss
them
How drunk are we to not realized how we've objectified our
women
Label them as dinner
Then blame them because of our male privilege when really
we know that they are the victims
And we act like it's all fine
We ignore the distressed signs
Till someone commits suicide
Then gives us 13 reasons why
This patriarchal society drove them not to be alive
It's time to realize we gotta uplift our women
Teach our young boys that they the queens of this earth that
we were given
And you treat royalty like more than just dirt we been tripping
They not just a hole for us to place our seeds
They the queen mother who nurtures those seeds till they grow
into trees
And we need trees cause they provide us with the oxygen to
breathe
It's a cycle
Black women are detrimental to our survival
We gotta treat them better

This Eurocentric Americanized system got us acting primitive
Its not cultural fitting
Black men have to stop perpetuating this illness its sickening
We cant fall into these sex symbol imagines
The media is killing us
Until we treat our women better our people will never
experience any liberational victory
It's a secret of our history
We've gotta see that they're royalty lets bring back some
chivalry
Men gotta stop treating women like objects please
Our legacy is the tradition of actions that we leave
It's time for us to fix these drunken thoughts we breathe

- *S.P.J.*

Dear Black Woman,

Sit down and be easy. Easy, Easy, just chill.
Let these heart rhymed words cater to you.
If you are queen, then sit on your throne
and let me clown in my entertainment.
Feel free to hate it, but know it's all in love
for you. I'm sure you'll find something that
makes your being move.

-   Jiggy Ellis

Fault

I'm a master of deception, keep these women with
questions,
searching for cruel intentions, in this flattering diction,
I'm the perfect depiction, a real life rendition,
the knight in shining armor, all the fairytales mention,
and just like them, I am a piece of fiction,
only real to those who are willing to listen, those women
insecure,
that all the movies forewarned, but they, didn't pay
attention,
all the music sang, women crying in pain,
with this many examples how could you get played,
is it cause your mother got beat and stayed,
or daddy wasn't around, and so you long for the day,
a man will come and treat you that way, make you feel like
a princess,
so you cling to the first man who calls you a sweet name,
and every time you moan his name, you release that built
up incest,
perverted longing for a father, you now allow yourself to be
caught up,
by this no good man, and who can you blame but yourself,
environmental product can no longer be your excuse,
when you know your problem, but refuse to change,
and I'm tired of hearing you complain, so stop it,
if it's okay for you, then I'm just a product of my

environment too,

so my actions with you don't knock it,

Disney taught me to save the damsel in distress,

learned game from Martin, Jamie King, and the Fresh Prince,

and I've seen the Government rape my family since before I could walk,

we can play this blame game all day long,

but it won't change shit, we are who we are,

and your lot may not have been the best pick, but Psalms 82:6 says

"ye are gods", therefore we have the ability to revolutionize our lives,

and this world, for our people built the great pyramids,

long before in the cotton fields we served,

no matter what has been stolen from us, no matter what has been hidden,

realize that you are the Gold of Africa,

and the proof lies in the melanin in your skin,

and if black Jesus died for this world sins,

so that we could have life, we should live ours to the fullest,

and I meant to write about how silly you women are,

but had to face my own man in the mirror, and realized I too am foolish,

so today I break these mentally enslaving chains, and in full consciousness say,

I AM SORRY THAT AS A AFRICAN KING

I ALLOWED THINGS TO GET THIS WAY

~J.E.

Chocolate

I just love chocolate,
I mean, even the thought of it
is captivating, think if
strawberry amazing
had chocolate on it,
or like it's been sitting
in the oven on two hundred,
surrounded by darkness
but furnaced by light,
melamarinating,
that for which God said
have patience, and set a place
for, to consider as your own soul,
the cistern of my eternal youth,
proof of my existence,
the gospel of my mission,
dammit,
chocolate is just so damn good,
the dribbles of its kiss
the heat of barbershops,
gold chocolate handed,
I could never flop,
but I wop, wonder over precision,
cause chocolate your definition
is a library of volumes,
if I could learn the wisdom
of your configuration, chocolate,

I could possibly make another you,
but chocolate, sweet chocolate,
you are enough

~J.E.

Sweepin

Would you believe in history,
if I told you it was a lie,
yeah you'd still believe it,
that you couldn't get over him,
though I'm going in with the charm,
you not even tryna give me an arm,
smiles and waves, like I'm miles away,
but I know you hope this love boat,
tired of backdoors and changed clothes,
want late holds yet not bold
enough to say what you quote,
chasing a cloak for mask that don't carry,
just a penguin cast of hurt facts,
you pray Hov will dust off your shoulders,
then maybe you can try again,
oh how your habits contend,
don't cough, just take it all in,
toot a boot and relax, get maxed
no need for mad, we can even get bad,
if you got energy to spend,
the time we could unravel
drinking on random rambles,
you probably can't handle,
scared from your play in shallow seas,
but you can laugh deeper,
love ain't that hard to find,
and easier an understanding,

if you could see

I only sweep talk,

in faith to teach your feet,

to walk and knock on what you need

~J.E.

A Call Away

You make me sick sometimes,
I just can't stand you,
wish I could reprimand you,
but like you say, "I ain't ya daddy",
and girl you a handful,
nothing I can't handle
or better yet tame,
someone gotta teach you how
to stay in the reins,
crossed and it's plain to see,
sitting at this red eye,
drunk in your anger, high on should be's,
teenage love affair turned unthinkable,
loving blind to its disease,
distance and time
doesn't mean anything
when she's on fire,
games hunger the arrows of a liar,
jimmy adventures of a boy
with big head but no genius,
and her fairly odd parents
can't answer her wish for more,
she's tired and she means it,
I'm worst cause I'm feeding,
promising better days,
with no faith that she'll see beyon
D

to everlasting,
no matter how much I feel her needs,
she only ordered me to fill,
so I heal at the best of what's required of me.

~J.E.

Saw

I knew you before all the glam and glitter,
before you got popping on twitter,
and stunting on the late night scene,
taking drinks with no receipt,
all for fun, it's just a wink,
they don't know that you don't sleep,
well they do thinking you're a red coupe,
but your head ain't chicken settled on eggs,
you wanna whip in a range
with aux on a flame, and it all in your name,
dodging last, thinking hyphens
cause your options are stifling,
dream nigga shade room trifling,
and I peep the secrets you ain't sharing,
reading your faces snapping your anguish,
cause it hurts more to hold it all in,
I remember your dependence
and think what a change,
when we'd share a plate just to get closer,
now you're tabled crossed from me
like your wallet wasn't chauffeured,
purse slacking compared to the allure,
you once weighed my balance,
now I see you're sawed by a game,
wish I could have made it back before

~J.E.

To Know

Your darkest moments matter nothing to a dark hole,

can consume anything when your mouth's not full,

meditate on time and space find the world still

moves, cause even if you stop

your lot can be pulled, sipping your poison,

heart eating frozen, yo grets got you sick and a fool,

why stick in the mud like the sun will never tirade,

day moon in a fade, and though biased

I'd say you the one,

but I mean who could do you better,

the way you wrap chances together,

look behind weather and somehow

ahead of the storm, bad to the bone

but no sin in your harmony,

an angel a thug will change life for,

but probably too late,

the ones you don't know if you hate

or hate you love, that

thin line Martin didn't dream of,

but I'd risk a dive in your pool,

race intoxication to your floor,

if I could just study the hieroglyphs

of your steps,

I'll learn the knowledge to cure

~J.E.

Try

I just want a woman who will try,
Not to change me into what she want,
when she barely know what she need,
cause her past left her on E,
when she had so many miles to go,
that'll squat not just for bun growth,
but to keep herself whole and healthy,
who waits on rich, to garner her wealth,
I just wanna take sides once
and we both be on the same page,
our minds be on the same shelf,
can Cudi in my rage, but
find peace on her moon,
escape from my gloom and
hide in her stealth,
camouflaging my pain till it's
unrecognizable, can we
love longer than the release of an iPhone,
or will we die fast like the battery,
can we endure, last, instead of finish first,
she could chain the medal of my heart,
but all I see is a pool of independent women,
and still no I in teamwork

~J.E.

Enough

I wanna find love before it's too late.
And at this point, all I want is the head
not the ache. To say hi,
without being maced by eyes
rolling sides in disdain.
Thinking my minds on her cake,
but my diet is plant based.
I prefer whole food,
cause my sweet tooth got
enough cavities, and the obesity got me
chopping off legs. Praying to God
I could lose my weights,
so I can fly to where he hides her.
Ready to test parted seas in chase.
And if I drown, let my sacrifice
make love more abound.
so when she looks she'll find,
the stone rolled out of place,
and be told,
that with head bowed I gave it up,
that the words would spread love,
that she may find peace in my touch,
that if she would just have faith,
I could be enough

~J.E.

Enemy

You are my enemy
so I calculate all the possibilities,
till the point I learn you
more than I know myself,
seeking out every flaw
and opportunity
to take advantage,
cause I can't afford a siege,
waiting day and night,
tryna make your walls breach,
I want to overcome you
in a moments notice,
but not when you sleep,
nor in a stab from the back,
I want you to see
the face of the man
that raised his flag at your surrender,
but I would never slave your subjects,
nor dishonor your throne,
cause I conquered this world,
and you were all that was left,
and I did all of this
just to get you,
so
I could give you my best

~J.E.

No More Games

I think I'm falling in love, and that's not hard to say
cause I'm saying it, but that shit is chilling,
like it causes me shivering, thinking on the sweet misery,
I mean like you map out this whole history,
and you come to a place where you gotta trust
someone to come into your space,
and not fuck it all up, like the white man
when he came to Africa and chained us all up,
and I refuse to be shackled just to breed or bread,
cause if we gonna make it through these seasons,
I need someone who knows how to spread,
who can win with her mind not her head,
yet still be salivating. Never weighing on maybes,
secure in my want for her needs to be filled,
that I'll piece together the legos,
building castles with moats for any sides
that'd try to boast a lie of divide,
jamming jukes, cause we'd never chance a rap,
texting 3000 goodbyes just to live in your lap,
facts you losing focus in this jungle
waiting for pigments to match,
I'm saying there's a future,
could you never look back?
cause i'll Kap a knee, even if it means
i'll never get to play, cause
what's the point of gaming life,
If you never reach the final stage

~J.E.

The End

Dominic "Nerd" McDonald is a Published Author; his first book is titled "The Love Song of D. Nerd McDonald". Dominic is a Los Angeles bred artist, who has since receiving his undergraduate degree consistently worked to bring his poetry and work to life for himself and his community.

Sean Cook is a Spoken Word artist who speaks from Inglewood who loves the Black community. Sean believes his words can be used to share our history, present passion, and speak to the future that lays ahead.

Edward Ellis is a Creative Writer who has self-published two books. Edward writes to connect with people. He uses his work as a means to share his experience, opinions, and soul.

Dear Reader,

H.E.R. is not a onetime read. We hope that you would write your own feelings in the pages that follow. What would you like to say to the black women that are around you? Do you have any adoration, encouragement, frustration, or love? Writing is a tool to express your own inner being. We look forward to the words you will share.

Thank You

FREE WRITE

Made in the USA
Lexington, KY
21 November 2019